Turtle's Boat

Written by Anke Hopkins

Illustrated by Deborah Brown

"Ride in my boat,"
said Turtle.

"Will it float?"
asked Rabbit.

The boat sank.

"Ride in my boat," said Turtle.

"Will it float?" asked Mouse.

The boat sank.

"Ride in my boat," said Turtle.

"Will it float?" asked Monkey.

"Yes, it will float,"
said Turtle.
And it did.